Bewilderment

PHOENIX POETS

DAVID FERRY

Bewilderment

New Poems and Translations

THE UNIVERSITY OF CHICAGO PRESS

Chicago & London

DAVID FERRY is the Sophie Chantal Hart Professor Emeritus of English at Wellesley College and also teaches at Suffolk University. In 2011 he received the prestigious Ruth Lilly Poetry Prize for his lifetime accomplishments.

The University of Chicago Press, Chicago 60637
The University of Chicago Press, Ltd., London
© 2012 by The University of Chicago
All rights reserved. Published 2012.
Printed in the United States of America
21 20 19 18 17 16 15 14 13 12   1 2 3 4 5

ISBN-13: 978-0-226-24488-4 (paper)
ISBN-13: 978-0-226-24490-7 (e-book)
ISBN-10: 0-226-24488-1 (paper)
ISBN-10: 0-226-24490-3 (e-book)

Library of Congress Cataloging-in-Publication Data
Ferry, David.
    Bewilderment : new poems and translations / David Ferry
        pages. cm. — (Phoenix poets)
    Includes bibliographical references.
    ISBN 978-0-226-24488-4 (paperback : alkaline paper)
    ISBN 0-226-24488-1 (paperback : alkaline paper)
    ISBN 978-0-226-24490-7 (e-book : alkaline paper)
    ISBN 0-226-24490-3 (e-book : alkaline paper)
    I. Title. II. Series: Phoenix poets.
    PS3556.E77B49 2012
    811'.54—dc23   2011050366

You lie in our bed as if an orchard were over us.
You are what's fallen from those fatal boughs.
Where will we go when they send us away from here?

CONTENTS

ACKNOWLEDGMENTS

Poems in this book have previously appeared, some in slightly different versions, in the following publications:

Daedalus: "October"

Literary Imagination and *The Word Exchange: Anglo-Saxon Poems in Translation* (W. W. Norton, 2011): "The Offering of Isaac (From *Genesis A*, Anglo Saxon)"

The New Yorker: "In the Reading Room," "Lake Water," and "Resemblance"

The Paris Review: "In Despair (Cavafy, "En Apognosi")," "Virgil, *Aeneid* VI, Lines 297–329" (as "Virgil, *Aeneid* VI), and "That Now Are Wild and Do Not Remember"

Poetry: "Ancestral Lines," "At the Street Corner (Rilke, "Das Lied des Zwerges")" (as "Song of the Little Cripple at the Street Corner"), "Coffee Lips," "The Departure from Fallen Troy (From Virgil, *Aeneid* II)" (as "Virgil, *Aeneid* II"), "Martial 1.101," "Incubus," "Catullus 11," "Scrim," "to where," and "Untitled Dream Poem" (as "Dream Poem")

Princetown Journal: "One Two Three Four Five"

A Public Space: "Anguilla (Eugenio Montale, "L'Anguilla")"

Raritan: "The Birds," "Measure 100," "Narcissus," and "Poem"

Slate: "The Intention of Things," "Soul," "The White Skunk," and "Turning Eighty-Eight, a Birthday Poem" in "Found Single-Line Poems" (as "Turning Eighty, a Birthday Poem")

The Threepenny Review: "Brunswick, Maine, Early Winter, 2000" (as "Brunswick, Maine"), "Street Scene," and "Willoughby Spit"

TriQuarterly: "Reading Arthur Gold's Poem 'Chest Cancer'"

The poems by Arthur R. Gold that appear in this book prefacing my poems about them are reprinted from his *Poems Written During a Period of Sickness* (Somerville, MA: Firefly Press, 1989). "Reading Arthur Gold's 'Trolley

One

NARCISSUS

There's the one about the man who went into
A telephone booth on the street and called himself up,
And nobody answered, because he wasn't home,
So how could he possibly have answered the phone?
The night went on and on and on and on.
The telephone rang and rang and nobody answered.

And there's the one about the man who went
Into the telephone booth and called himself up,
And right away he answered, and so they had
A good long heart-to-heart far into the night.
The sides of the phone booth glittered and shone in the light
Of the streetlight light as the night went echoing on.

Out in the wild hills of suburban New Jersey,
Up there above South Orange and Maplewood,
The surface of a lonely pond iced over,
Under the avid breath of the winter wind,
And the snow drifted across it and settled down,
So at last you couldn't tell that there was a pond.

FOUND SINGLE-LINE POEMS

Turning Eighty-Eight, a Birthday Poem:

    It is a breath-taking, near-death, experience.

Found poem:

    You ain't seen Nothing yet.

Found poem:

    We're all in this apart.

A Subtitle:

    Playing With My Self

ONE TWO THREE FOUR FIVE

anger

Anger is what I don't know what to do with.
I know it was anger was the trouble that other time.
I don't know where the anger came from, that time,
Or where it was I was going on anger's back
On a mission to somewhere to get me through the danger.

whatever

Whatever it is I think I probably know.
However whatever it is I keep from knowing.
No, it is not whatever I think I know.
Maybe I'll never know whatever it is.
Some day it has to be figured out. Whatever.

somebody

Somebody's got to tell me the truth some day.
And if somebody doesn't tell me the truth I'll tell it.
On my block there was somebody knew the truth, I think.
Or so I thought. Anyway somebody knew
That trying to tell the truth is looking for somebody.

isn't

If it isn't anywhere I guess it isn't.
But if it isn't why do I think it is?
I guess there really isn't any way
For me to find out what is or isn't there
In the black night where it either was or wasn't.

where

Where was it I was looking in the past?
It isn't where I've looked, that's no surprise.
I don't know what or where it is or was.
But maybe it isn't so much the where but the why.
Or maybe I haven't found it because beware.

SOUL

What am I doing inside this old man's body?
I feel like I'm the insides of a lobster,
All thought, and all digestion, and pornographic
Inquiry, and getting about, and bewilderment,
And fear, avoidance of trouble, belief in what,
God knows, vague memories of friends, and what
They said last night, and seeing, outside of myself,
From here inside myself, my waving claws
Inconsequential, wavering, and my feelers
Preternatural, trembling, with their amazing
Troubling sensitivity to threat;
And I'm aware of and embarrassed by my ways
Of getting around, and my protective shell.
Where is it that she I loved has gone to, as
This cold sea water's washing over my back?

UNTITLED

without

not any

THE INTENTION OF THINGS

The death that lives in the intention of things
To have a meaning of some sort or other,

That means to come to something in the end,
It is the death that lives not finding the meaning

Of this or that object as it moves among them
Uncertainly, moving among the shadows,

The things that are like shadows, shadows of things,
The things the shadows of shadows, all in the effort

To put off the death that we are coming to.
The intention makes its way among its moments,

Choosing this object or that, uncertainly,
Somebody's body or the leaves of a tree

On a summer night in a landscape somewhere else,
Under which something happened that made it different.

It is seeking to find the meaning of what they are.
But it moves uncertainly among them, the shadows,

The things that are like shadows, putting off
The death that is coming, that we are coming to.

It is the death that lives that makes the flower
Be what it's going to be and makes it die,

And makes the musical phrase complete itself,
Or fail to complete itself, as Goethe said,

Writing a friend whose son had died in the Army:
"So you have had another terrible trial.

It's still, alas, the same old story: to live
Long is to outlive many; and after all,

We don't even know, then, what it was all about.
The answer to part of the riddle is, we each

Have something peculiarly our own, that we
Mean to develop by letting it take its course.

This strange thing cheats us from day to day, and so
We grow old without knowing how it happened or why."

It is the death that lives in the intention of things
To have a meaning of some sort or other;

Implacable, bewildered, it moves among us
Seeking its own completion, still seeking to do so,

But also putting it off, oh putting it off,
The death that is coming, that we are coming to.

YOUR PERSONAL GOD

From Horace, *Epistles* II.2 (lines 180–89)

Jewels, marble, ivory, paintings, beautiful Tuscan
Pottery, silver, Gaetulian robes dyed purple—
Many there are who'd love to have all of these things.
There are some who don't care about them in the least.
Why one twin brother lives for nothing but pleasure,
And loves to fool around even more than Herod
Loves his abundant gardens of date-trees, while
The other twin brother works from morning to night
Improving his farm, ploughing and clearing the lands,
Pruning and planting, working his ass off, only
The genius knows, the personal god who knows
And controls the birth star of every person
There is in the world. Your personal god is the god
Who dies in a sense when your own breath gives out,
And yet lives on, after you die, to be
The personal god of somebody other than you;
Your personal god, whose countenance changes as
He looks at you, smiling sometimes, sometimes not.

Two

DEDICATION TO HIS BOOK

Catullus 1, to Cornelius Nepos

Who is it I should give my little book to,
So pretty in its pumice-polished covers?

Cornelius, I'll give my book to you:
Because you used to think my nothings somethings,

At the time when you were the first in Italy
To dare to write our whole long history,

Three volumes, under the sign of Jupiter,
Heroically achieved; so take this little

Book of mine for what it's worth; whatever;
And oh, patroness Virgin, grant that it shall

Live and survive beyond the century.

BRUNSWICK, MAINE, EARLY WINTER, 2000

That day when Suzie drove us out to get
The lobsters at the lobster place at the cove:

Bill Moran in the passenger seat of the car,
Doubled up as if in a fit of laughter,

A paroxysm of helpless, silent laughter,
At the joke the Parkinson's had played on him.

The big joke he simply couldn't get over.

———

Bill Moran at breakfast time, in the kitchen,
Bent double in his wheelchair, his chin almost

Touching the kitchen table, and his eyes
Intently studying a piece of toast,

A just discovered, as yet unreadable
Mesopotamian language, not related

To Akkadian or Sumerian, much older
Even than what he knew about already—

The great old man with his ferocity
Of tenderness and joy, his eyes intently

Studying the text. He sent me once
A passage copied from Nietzsche's book *Daybreak*:

"It is a connoisseurship of the word;
Philology is that venerable art

That asks one thing above all other things:
Read slowly, slowly. It is a goldsmith's art,

Looking before and after, cautiously;
Considering; reconsidering;

Studying with delicate eyes and fingers.
It does not easily get anything done."

Bill looking for heaven on the tabletop.

———

After the funeral Suzie said, "Bill thought
He'd be flying around up there somewhere forever."

And he could fly. After breakfast that day
We wheeled him away from the kitchen table and into

The living room and there was a frame contraption
Set up on long thin crane-like legs. It looked

Like something in a children's playground, with
A canvas sling to carry him through the air

From the wheelchair to another chair; heartbreaking,
Swaddled, small, ridiculously like

A newborn baby. Or else the sling resembled
Those slings you see on television when

They rescue people from their sinking boats
And carry them up under the angel wings

To safety in the helicopter noise.

He, who had been the one to whom I had
Recited my poems and then he wrote them down
With his faithful scribal hand for which already
He was well known and had been justly praised,
Demetrius has died. He lived to be
Fifteen years old, and after that four summers.
Even the Caesars had heard how good he was.

When he fell sick and I knew he was going to die,
I didn't want him to descend to where
The Stygian shades are, still a slave, and so
I relinquished my ownership of him to his sickness.
Deserving by my deed to have gotten well,
He knew what I had done and was grateful for it,
Calling me his patron, falling free,

Down to those waters that are waiting there.

MEASURE 100

There is a passage in the Mozart K.
511 Rondo in A Minor,

Measures 98 through 101,
And focused on measure 100, where there are

At least four different melodies, or fragments
Of melodies, together and apart,

Resolving themselves, or unresolving themselves
With enigmatic sweetness, or melancholy;

Or distant memories of victories,
Personal, royal, or mythic over demons;

Or sophisticated talking about ideas;
Or moments of social or sexual concord; or

Of parting though with mutual regret;
Or differences and likenesses of natures;

It was what you said last night, whoever you are,
That told me what your nature is, and didn't;

It was the way that you said the things you said;
Grammar and syntax, agents of our fate;

Allusions to disappointments; as also to
An unexpected gift somebody gave

To someone there in the room behind the music;
Or somebody else working out a problem

At a table under the glowing light of a lamp;
Or the moment when the disease has finally

Proceeded to its foregone working through,
Leaving behind it nothing but the question

Of whether there's a heaven to sing about.
The clarity and poise of the arrangement,

The confidence in the very writing of it,
Fosters the erroneous impression that

There's all the truth there is, in the little nexus,
Encapsulated here in narratives

Diminutive in form; perfectly told,
As far as they are willing to be told.

According to the dictionary, "resolve"
Derives from "solve" and "solve" derives from the Latin

"*Solvere*" that means "untie," and "*re-*"
Is an intensifier, meaning "again,"

And so, again, again, and again, what's tied
Must be untied again, and again, and again;

Or else it's like what happens inside a lock,
The cylinders moving back and forth as the lock

Is locked, unlocked, and locked, over and over.

ANCESTRAL LINES

It's as when following the others' lines,
Which are the tracks of somebody gone before,
Leaving me mischievous clues, telling me who

They were and who it was they weren't,
And who it is I am because of them,
Or, just for the moment, reading them, I am;

Although the next moment I'm back in myself, and lost.
My father at the piano saying to me,
"Listen to this, he called the piece *Warum*?"

And the nearest my father could come to saying what
He made of that was lamely to say he didn't,
Schumann didn't, my father didn't, know why.

"What's in a dog's heart"? I once asked in a poem,
And Christopher Ricks when he read it said "Search me."
He wasn't just being funny, of course; he was right.

You can't tell anything much about who you are
By exercising on the Romantic bars.
What *are* the wild waves saying? I don't know.

And Shelley didn't know, and knew he didn't.
In his great poem, "Ode to the West Wind." he
Said that the leaves of his pages were blowing away,

Dead leaves, like ghosts from an enchanter fleeing.

ENTREATY

Make me thy liar, even as the forest is.

OCTOBER

The day was hot, and entirely breathless, so
The remarkably quiet remarkably steady leaf fall
Seemed as if it had no cause at all.

The ticking sound of falling leaves was like
The ticking sound of gentle rainfall as
They gently fell on leaves already fallen,

Or as, when as they passed them in their falling,
Now and again it happened that one of them touched
One or another leaf as yet not falling,

Still clinging to the idea of being summer:
As if the leaves that were falling, but not the day,
Had read, and understood, the calendar.

SPRING

From Virgil, *Georgics* II (lines 323–45)

It's spring that adorns the woods and groves with leaves;
In spring the soil, desiring seed, is tumid,
And then the omnipotent father god descends
In showers from the sky and enters into
The joyful bridal body of the earth,
His greatness and her greatness in their union,
Bringing to life the life waiting to live.
Birdsong is heard in every secluded thicket,
And all the beasts of the field have become aware
That love's appointed days have come again.
The generous earth is ready to give birth
And the meadows ungirdle for Zephyr's warming breezes;
The tender dew is there on everything;
The new grass dares entrust itself to the new
Suns of the new days and the little tendrils
Of the young vines have no fear of a South Wind coming
Nor of a North Wind from a stormy sky;
The vine brings forth its buds; its leaves unfold.
I think it must have been that just such days
As these were the shining days when the world was new;
Everywhere it was spring, the whole world over;
The East Wind held in check its winter winds;
The beasts drank in the light of that first dawn;
The first men, born of the earth, raised up their heads
From the stony ground; the woods were stocked with game,
And the first stars came out in the sky above.
Nor could the tender plants endure their lot
If spring's relief were not to intervene
Between the heat of summer and winter's cold.

ANGUILLA

Eugenio Montale, "L'Anguilla"

Anguilla, eel, sea-siren
That making its way from those
Cold Baltic seas to get to ours,
Our estuaries, deltas,
And into our streams, and from
The profound beneath the river rises up
Against the downstream impetus of flow,
Upstream from branch to branch, and into ever
Smaller capillaries, seeking ever
Evermore to enter
Into the heart of rock, inching through mire,
Until, one afternoon, a flash of light,
Ricocheted off a sun-struck chestnut leaf,
Glints upon the surface
Of a stagnant pool
Or in a dry runnel coming down the side
Of the Apennines,
Down to Romagna; eel, sea-siren,
Candleblink, whiplash, arrow of love,
Which only our arid ditches or
The desiccated Pyrenean vacant streambeds can
Show the way back
To the paradise of fecundation;
Green soul, searching for life
Where only desolation and
Absolute driedupness are;
Scintilla, spark, whose declaration is

That all begins when all is burned to charcoal;
Buried-dead-tree-stump;
Brief-iris-rainbow-glint,
Twin to the one that, eyelash-framed,
Sets you shining intact among the sons of men
Sunk in your mire;

Do you not see that she is your sister?

IN THE READING ROOM

Alone in the library room, even when others
Are there in the room, alone, except for themselves,
There is the illusion of peace; the air in the room

Is stilled; there are reading lights on the tables,
Looking as if they're reading, looking as if
They're studying the text, and understanding,

Shedding light on what the words are saying;
But under their steady imbecile gaze the page
Is blank, patiently waiting not to be blank.

The page is blank until the mind that reads
Crosses the black river, seeking the Queen
Of the Underworld, Persephone, where she sits

By the side of the one who brought her there from Enna,
Hades the mute, the deaf, king of the dead letter;
She is clothed in the beautiful garment of our thousand

Misunderstandings of the sacred text.

Three

COFFEE LIPS

The guest who came in to the street people's suppers last night,
An elderly man with a lost smart little boy's face and a look

As if he might turn against you anytime soon,
As if he'd just come into this world and he was extremely

Wary about what the world was going to be, and he said,
"If I ask you a question will you give me a truthful answer?"

And I said, "That depends on what the question is,"
Thinking the little elderly boy looked sophisticated and

As if he'd in fact been a long time in the world
And would get the tone right, and maybe he did, or maybe he didn't;

At any rate he went on to ask the question,
"When I come into places like this and there are people holding

Coffee cups to their lips and they look at me,
Are they about to drink the coffee or not to drink the coffee?"

He was balancing the world on the tip of his witty unknowing nose.
I felt like I was falling down someplace else than anywhere there.

INCUBUS

at the supper for street people

The young man who goes all muffled up from harm
With whatever he has found, newspaper pages
Carefully folded to make a weirdly festive
Hat or hood, down almost over his eyes,

Everything carefully arranged to make him other.
The paper-covered razorblade in his mouth,
Or the bit of wood, like carrying a message.
A fantasy so clever, outwitting itself,

That it became what it was he was, and so
He was what it was. The long loose shirt too big
For him, the pantaloons too big for him,
Loose like the pantaloons of the circus clown,

Some kind of jacket too big, he got it somewhere.
His burden slept dreaming everywhere upon him.
As if his whole body and his clothes were dreaming
Of his condition and the dream came true.

His clothes slept on him as if they were his lover.

AT THE STREET CORNER

Rilke, "Das Lied des Zwerges"

Maybe my soul's all right.
But my body's all wrong,
All bent and twisted.
It's this that hurts me so.

My soul keeps trying, trying
To straighten my body up.
It hangs on my skeleton, frantic,
Flapping its terrified wings.

Look here, look at my hands,
They look like little wet toads
After a rainstorm's over,
Hopping, hopping, hopping.

Maybe God didn't like
The look on my face when He saw it.
Sometimes, a big dog
Looks right into it.

THE LATE-HOUR POEM

In an hour of furious clarity,
By liquor made,
Full of a fierce charity,
My harp I played!

I made a loud uproar!
I went in turn
From door to every door.
Marry or burn!

Love your neighbor! I cried.
Pity the poor
Divided people, who side
By side here lie,

Transfixed in sleep; and shadow
Covers each eye!
On house and house the echo
Rang and rebounded.

My harp made everybody know
How brave I sounded!

AT A BAR

While in a bar I bore
Indignity with those
Others whose hearts were sore
Or sour or sick or such
As made them humankind,
I looked into my glass
To see if I could find
Something to give me ease.

Narcissus at the pool,
I looked lovingly at
My own disordered fool,
Who would not tell me much.
But stared patiently back.
He would not tell me what
I'd ever have or lack
He would not tell me that.

I looked along the bar
And saw my fellow creature
Bravely standing there.
"By word, sign, or touch,"
I cried, in my mute heart,
"Tell me, be my teacher,
Be learnèd in that art,
What is my name and nature?"

My pulse ticked in my wrist;
The noon hung around unawares;
Outside the traffic passed.
Like quiet cattle or such,
Standing about a pool,
Dumb ignorant creatures,
My fellow, my self, my fool,
Ignorant of our natures.

TO VARUS

Horace, *Odes* 1.18

For planting in the rich Tiburtine soil
Upon the slopes of Mt. Catillus, Varus,
Favor no plant before the sacred vine.
Bacchus commands that everything be hard
For him who abstains from wine, and Bacchus says
The troubles that wear away our days are not
Made easier by any other means.
After a drink or two who is it who
Complains about the hardships of his lot—
His poverty, or his service in the army?
Who fails to praise you then, O father Bacchus?
Who fails to praise you too, O queen of love?
And yet there is a lesson in the example
Of the fight between the Centaurs and the Lapiths,
That went so far too far at the drunken banquet,
And there's another in the Sithonian drinkers
Who think they tell right from wrong by squinting along
The disappearing line libidinous desire
Draws on the wet bartop. I would not dare
To stir you up, O Bacchus, against your will,
Nor will I be the one to betray to the light
The secret signs that you have covered over
In grape and ivy leaves. Bacchus, repress
The cymbal and the Berecynthian horn
And those who revel in that raucous music:
Blind love that has no eyes but for itself;
Vain Glory with its vacant head held high;
And barfly Faithlessness whose promiscuous tongue
Spills all its secrets into promiscuous ears.

SOMEBODY IN A BAR

after Edward Hopper

The veined hand like a stitched glove
On the bar left lying;
The bold brow, bald, bare
To the bare bulb's black glare;
Slope-shouldered, unready;

This starer into the mirror
Over the bar; this mirror
The transformer into horror,
Into terror of what whose habit is
To be by daylight pain

Merely; dull repeater; drudger;
Trudger on the treadmill of the nerves;
The innocence of animals drinks here,
Here at this lonely pool the poor beast drinks.

IN DESPAIR

Cavafy, "En Apognosi"

He's gone from him forever,
his lips on the lips of every
wanting to fool himself
lips of the boy he gave
But he's gone from him forever,

and ever since he's sought
boy he goes to bed with,
into thinking those are the very
himself to, long ago.
he's never coming back.

He's gone from him forever
because, he said, he wanted
pleasure, unnatural pleasure
the shameful pleasure he wanted
There was still time, he said,

as if he never was,
to save himself from the shameful
of what they did together,
to save his body from.
to save himself, he said.

He's gone from him forever,
He seeks, hallucinating,
on the lips of other boys
that shameful pleasure he'd had

as if he never was.
self-deluding, seeking
the lips of him with whom
he'll never have again.

DIDO IN DESPAIR

From Virgil, *Aeneid* IV (lines 450–73)

Then, truly, wretched Dido, overwhelmed
By knowledge of the fate that has come upon her,
Prays for death; she is weary of looking at
The overarching sky. And to make sure
That what has been begun will be completed
And that she will depart from the light, she saw
As she set out her ritual offerings
Upon the incense-burning altars, how—
The horror!—the holy water darkened and
The wine was changed to an excremental slime.
She said nothing about this, no, not even to
Her sister. Furthermore, within her palace
There was a marble chapel devoted to
Her husband who had died, and which she had
Wonderfully and faithfully maintained,
Adorning it with leaves and snow-white garlands.
At night, when night possessed the world, she heard,
When she was there, noises that sounded like
Her husband's voice, words calling to her; and too,
She heard the gloomy sound of the owl alone
Upon the city roofs, in long-continued
Wailing lamentation; sometimes she heard
The voices of old sayings of the prophets,
Speaking to her in her head their terrible warnings.
And in her sleep savage Aeneas himself
Drives her before him in her madness; or
Always alone along some vacant street
Unendingly unaccompanied she seeks

To find her Tyrians in an empty land—
It's as when Pentheus, demented, sees
The Furies and, seeing double, sees two suns,
And see two Thebes, two cities, or as when
Agamemnon's son Orestes flees from his mother,
Who is brandishing fire and writhing snakes, and there
In the doorway the Dirae crouch, and patiently wait.

CATULLUS II

Little sparrow,

      my girlfriend's pet delight,

dandling you in her lap,

      or letting you

peck at her finger,

      or getting you

even to bite it,

      A little bit sharply,

when she,

      who's the light of my love,

still feels

      like playing with you,

like that,

      and doing so

in the aftermath

      of the quieting down

of her earlier ardor,

      in order to

relieve what's left of it

      —ah, I wish

I could play

      with you,

just like that,

      until,

at last,

      that would make me

feel

      a lot better.

VIRGIL, *AENEID* II

Lines 250–67

And now the heavens move and night comes in
And covers with its darkness earth and sky
And the tricks of the Myrmidons. Throughout the city
The Trojans, wearied by joy, lie fast asleep;
And now the Greeks set out from Tenedos,
Their ships in ordered formation, under the silent
Light of the friendly moon, making their way
Quietly toward the shore they know so well,
And when the lead ship's beacon light is shown,
Sinon, protected by the complicit fates,
Furtively opens up its wooden side,
And frees the Achaeans from the Horse's womb.
The Horse releases them to the open air
And joyfully they come out. First come the captains
Thessander, and Sthenelus, and dire Ulysses,
Lowering themselves to the ground by means of a rope,
And Ácamas, Thoas, and Neoptólemus of
The house of Peleus, and Machaón the prince,
And Menelaus, and Epéus, he
Who built the Wooden Horse. They enter the city,
That slumbers submerged in wine and sleep; they surprise,
And quietly kill, the watchmen, and open the gates
To welcome in their comrades from the fleet,
Letting them in for what they are going to do.

THERMOPYLAE

Cavafy, "Thermopylae"

Honor is due to those who are keeping watch,
Sentinels guarding their own Thermopylae;
Never distracted from what is right to do,
And right to be; in all things virtuous,
But never so hardened by virtue as not to be

Compassionate, available to pity;
Generous if they're rich, but generous too,
Doing whatever they can, if they are poor;
Always true to the truth, no matter what,
But never scornful of those who have to lie.

Even more honor is due when, keeping watch,
They see that the time will come when Ephialtes
Will tell the secret to the Medes and they
Will know the way to get in through the goat-path.

Four

STREET SCENE

Someone's shadow and the shadow of his dog
Are what I see through my window looking out
Across the street. Someone's shadow, and then
As the leaves of the tree that's just outside my window
Move a little, this way, or that, with the breeze,
It's Mr. Wrenn, taking his dog for a walk,
Or being out there with his dog, in order, maybe,
To be seen as one of us; the two of them,
Standing there, vacant of conversation;
His tan shirt, brown pants, bald spot, his trivial pug
Absurdly the color of a golden retriever.

That this huge stage presenteth nought but shows

The red truck that was parked in the parking lot
That they have walked past without seeming to notice it,
Is now leaving the parking lot. It is as if
The man and his dog, both of them, knew that the truck
Was going to move, because all three of them have
Become, in common, elements of the scene
That I'm observing, and so all three of them seem
To understand that they have a common purpose.
The side of the red truck just a moment ago
Had, painted on it in white graphics, CHARETTE.
That word was on it when it left my view.
Now, a blue truck with no letters on its side,
So giving no information about its purpose,
Turns into the parking lot and then backs into
The same slot under the overhang of the building.

A shifting of the leaves that I'm looking through
Prevents me from seeing who gets out of the truck
And where it is he goes. It is as if
The brilliant red truck with the white letters on it,
Outside my range of sight had changed its color,

Whereon the stars in secret influence comment,

And therefore it is as if I had imagined
The change of color, the vanishing of the one truck,
The sudden appearance of the other one.
Magic. A trick of magic performed by me,
Something that I performed because I saw it;
Or the trick was performed by the unseen hand of the world.
CHARETTE went out of business in that instant.
And what became of Mr. Wrenn and his dog?
Hurled down to the Underworld, twisting and turning,
The two of them falling, the dog's leash fluttering
In the eerie light down there through which they fall.

WILLOUGHBY SPIT

The little fence around the tiny front yard
Seemed very little even to a child.

Even as a child, visiting there from the North
For a week or maybe two weeks every summer,

I experienced the place as if I had been reading
In a book that was written for very young children to read,

Vivid, crude, charming, frightening in the way
It simplified some truth about the world

You didn't know enough to know about.
There were a few flowers in the little front yard,

Ineptly shaped by nature, looking as if
Someone in a hurry had stuck them in the sand.

There were some boards for getting across the sand
From the gate to the front porch steps. The boards were burning

Under your feet with an intensity
That took your breath away. It was so hot

You could smell the heat of the old gray boards
Of the little walk and the fence as if they might

Burst into smokeless flame at any moment.
The sand of the beach across the street was dark.

It was a surprise to step on it and find
That it was burning dry, although in fact

The flat dull waters of the bay had been
Known to rise up in rage and smite the shore

And get all the way to the road that divided the Spit
And even across it, and even across the sand

On the other side of the road, almost to reach
The smaller bay beyond. The other houses

Were mostly those of strangers, though of course
Not all of them were strangers to Aunt Nellie,

But hardly any were friends since she was bound
Within the spell her eccentricity drew

Like a magic circle around her in the sand,
So none might enter. In the sands behind the houses

There were scrub pines, and living in the woodshed
Behind Aunt Nellie's house were black widow spiders,

So I was told. In the little dark parlor of the house
There was an upright piano, table lamps

With lampshades with beads along their lower edges;
There was a rocker, made of some very dark wood,

Varnished almost black; a couple of other armchairs,
High-backed, perhaps of the same wood but

With needlepoint-covered seats, and one of them
With needlepoint oval insets on the arms;

On a table, a newspaper, called (I think) the Pilot,
Telling, perhaps, the story of how a drunken

Sailor on the roller coaster that used
To tower high above the other attractions

At Ocean View Amusement Park nearby
Like the skeleton of a dinosaur

Had stood up just as the car tipped over the highest
Point of the highest loop and how he fell

Straight down to his death while the car plunged down
On its thrilling tracks, entirely unconcerned.

Or else it was from a Ferris wheel that he fell,
Just as the wheel had brought him to the top,

And when he stood up the footboard under his feet
Seemed to rock back and forward and back and forward,

Then poured him out over and down, a little figure
Vividly clear as he fell in the story I heard,

Of a roller coaster or Ferris wheel back then.
How long ago the sailor must have forgotten

The manner of his death. On the piano were
Some pages of sheet music. "In the gloaming,

Oh my darling, when the lights are burning low,
And the shadows of the evening softly come

And softly go." In the summer heat the door in
From the front porch was always a little bit open

But the light from outside got only a little way in.
On another table a candy dish or ashtray

Decorated with a woman's head, with marcelled
Golden hair and a Grecian profile, expressing

Some noble outrage or otherwise disturbed
Emotion, for example, catastrophic loss.

There was a curtain, beaded also, I think,
Between the living room and the dining room

That loomed in littleness beyond. There was a huge
Dining room table and a huge sideboard,

The two of them so big you'd have thought the room
Had to be built around them to get them in,

Inherited long ago from a larger house,
Or a wedding present with larger expectations.

And next to this was the dark bedroom in which
Aunt Nellie and her husband, Uncle Frank,

Slept together in sexless affection, as if
In secret collusion. On the bedroom dresser

There was a hairnet, a box containing pins,
Straight pins and safety, mixed in with jewelry—

Brooches, and earrings, bracelets, and other such things.
They glinted in the darkness of the room.

In the sand out back of the house there were those little
Black (or dark purple) pods or podlike things,

Some kind of seaweed which, on the beach up North,
In New Jersey, I liked to pick up and burst

Between my fingers. But here, because of the spiders,
They reminded me of them and I didn't touch them.

Aunt Nellie's picture was in the paper once,
Triumphantly posing with a large bottle,

Black widow spiders inside looking out,
As conscious as fireflies of their situation.

EVERYBODY'S TREE

The storm broke over us on a summer night,
All brilliance and display; and being out,
Dangerously I thought, on the front porch standing,
Over my head the lightning skated and blistered
And sizzled and skidded and yelled in the bursting down
Around my maybe fourteen-years-old being,
And in spite of all the fireworks up above
And what you'd thought would have been the heat of all
That exuberant rage, the air was suddenly cool
And fresh and as peaceable as could be,
Down on the porch, so different from what it was
My body was expecting. The raindrops on
The front porch railing arms peacefully dripped
As if they weren't experiencing what
Was coming down from above them as an outrage.
My body could reinterpret it as a blessing,
Being down there in the cool beneath the heat.
It wasn't of course being blessed but being suddenly
Singled out with a sense of being a being.

Sometime early on in the nineteenth century,
Down in the part of New Jersey called New Sweden,
Someone with some familial link to me,
Maybe a grandsire down a maternal line,
Whose name was Isaiah Toy, was sitting up
In the house of his dying bachelor uncle, who
Was also Isaiah Toy, and Isaiah Toy,
His uncle, would leave his farm to Isaiah Toy,
His nephew, who was sitting in a chair

In the next room to where his uncle was dying.
I don't know what kind of light it would have been
That he was reading the Bible by while his uncle
Slept toward leaving the farm to him, when suddenly,
Reading, who was it, Matthew, or maybe Mark,
The glory of the Lord broke over his head,
Or so he said. Methodists got excited when
In the woods of their confusion suddenly
The moonlight burst above their heads and they
Were ever after then enlightened beings.
"Light suddenly broke upon his mind. For fear
Of disturbing his dying uncle with his joy,
The expression of which he could not repress, he went
Out of the house into the brilliant moonlight
Shining upon the snow, and gave vent to his feelings,
Shouting 'Glory to God! Glory to God in the Highest.'"

Coming back in from the porch, while the storm went on
Above our little house, I went to close the window
Of the dining room that looked out back of the house
And I could see, could dimly see, the backs
Of the Bowdoin Street houses all in a row,
Occasionally lit up and washed blank by
Downpours of the lightning of the storm:
The Beckers' house, the Gileses' house, the Demarests',
Jean Williams's where she lay in "the sleeping-sickness."
And Bessie Phelps's house, the one next to hers,
The property lines of the houses and their yards
Made briefly briefly clear by the lightning flashing.
Running along the back of the hither yards
Was a tiny ditch defining the property lines
Between where our Yale Street backyards ended
And where the yonder Bowdoin Street houses' backyards
Backed up to it; my childhood fantasy thought

The waterless tiny ditch was the vestige of
A mysterious long ago bygone vanished river
That came from somewhere else and went somewhere.
I don't know, didn't know, though of course I knew them,
Whatever went on in those houses, or in my mind,
Or my mother's mind, or my father's, asleep upstairs,
Though I kept wondering, and wonder still,
What is it they were doing? Who were they?
All, all, are gone, the unfamiliar faces.

Over beyond in the night there was a houseless
Wooded lot next door to Bessie's house;
Because of the houselessness and because of the trees,
I could think of it as a forest like the forest
In Hawthorne's great short story "Young Goodman Brown,"
And from out that window looking out at the back
I could faintly see, or thought I could see,
Maybe once or twice, by a flash, a raining gust
Of the light of lightning, the waving tops of trees
In that empty wooded lot beyond Bessie's house.
The houseless tiny lot seemed like a forest
And in the forest there was a certain tree
Which all of us children somehow knew was known
As Everybody's Tree, so it was called,
Though nobody knew who it was who gave it its name;
And on the smooth hide of its trunk there were initials,
Nobody knew who it was who had inscribed them.
We children had never gathered around that tree
To show each other our bodies.
                        I remember how
Crossing through that houseless wooded lot,
On my way home on an autumn afternoon,
That strange tree, with the writing on it, seemed

Ancient, a totem, a rhapsody playing a music
Written according to an inscrutable key.
How did I ever know what the tree was called?
Somebody must have told me. I can't remember.
Whoever it was has become a shade imagined
From an ancient unrecoverable past.

Five

THE OFFERING OF ISAAC

From *Genesis A*, Anglo-Saxon

Then the Lord wanted to know
      How steadfast was his man,
So He said, in the Lord's stern voice,
      "Abraham, Abraham, you
Must take your belovèd child,
      Your own, your only son,
And go with him to where
      I will show you what to do.
A place there is, high in the hills.
      You must climb up there on foot.
The two of you together,
      Around you only nothing,
Only the mountain peaks
      Around you witnessing.
And there make ready a fire,
      A bale-fire for your bairn,
And then, you must, yourself,
      Take up the sword you carry,
And kill him with its edge,
      And burn his dear body black
In the flames you have set going
      And present what you have done,
A burnt offering to Me."

      Abraham heard the Lord
And did not put off the journey.
      At once he made his way,
Determined and intent
      On the task that he had been

Commanded to undertake.
    He was in awe of the Word
Of the Lord God of angels.
    He was the Lord's servant,
Eager to please his Master.
    Blessèd was Abraham.
Without any night-rest
    He got up from his bed.
He obeyed without any question
    The commandment of the Lord.
He girded on his sword,
    Fear of the Lord's Word
Continual in his breast.
    That good old man, the giver
Of rings to his followers,
    He harnessed and bridled his asses,
And selected from his household
    Two young men, and told them
To go with him on his journey.
    Isaac his half-grown son
Was the third one of the party.
    He was himself the fourth.
So together they went to do
    The bidding of the Lord,
Hastening on their way
    Across the deserted landscape,
Until, on the third day,
    The bright light of the morning
Rose up from the deep water,
    Where everything begins.

There, then, the blessèd man
    Looked up and saw the high
Mountain that the Lord

Had told him they were to go to.
Abraham spoke to the two
      Retainers and said, "My men,
Stay here where we have camped.
      We will return when we
Have carried out what the King
      Of Souls has told us to do."
Then Abraham left them and went
      Up onto the high mountain,
Climbing through woods and groves,
      Taking his own son with him.
The son carried the wood,
      The father carried the fire,
And was carrying the sword.
      Then his belovèd son,
Trudging beside his father,
      Said to his father, "Father,
We're carrying the wood,
      The fire, and the sword,
To do what the bright Lord
      Asks us to do, but where
Is the sacrificial victim?
      Where is the offering
To put upon the fire"?
      His father, who was steadfast,
Faithful to what the Creator
      Had told him to do, replied
"He, who is the true
      King, the Guardian,
Protector of His people,
      He will find what is right
And what is fitting for this."
      Then, obedient, resolute,
Steadfast, he went on climbing

Up the steep mountain with
His only son beside him,
        Until they came to the top,
To the place to which the Lord
        Had told him where to go,
And there he took the sticks
        Of wood his son had carried
And with them made ready the fire,
        Only the mountains around,
Witnessing what he was doing.
        Hand and foot he bound
His own, his only son,
        Young half-grown Isaac,
And lifted his own child up
        And laid him on the pyre,
And took up the sword in his hand
        And stood there ready to kill him,
And for the thirsty fire
        To drink the blood of his boy.

Then suddenly from above
        An angel of the Lord
Called out to Abraham
        In a loud voice, "Abraham!"
Abraham stood still,
        He stood stock-still and listened
And heard the words of the angel.
        "Abraham, do not kill
Your own, your only son.
        Take him up, lift him away
From the pyre you have put him upon.
        The Lord has granted him
Great honor, and you, great scion,
        And patriarch of the Hebrews,

Will be given many rewards
> By the Guardian of Souls,
Because you were willing to
> Sacrifice your son,
Your belovèd only son,
> In obedience to the Lord
And for the love of Him."
> The fire went on burning.

The Creator of Mankind
> Had so approved the heart
Of Abraham, Lot's kinsman,
> That God gave him back his bairn
In safety, and alive.
> Then Abraham, the brother
Of Haran, turned his head,
> And looked back over his shoulder,
And saw, not far away,
> A ram caught in the brambles.
Then he took hold of the ram
> And quickly lifted it up
Onto the burning pyre
> And took his sword and killed it,
In place of his own son,
> There on the smoking altar
Stained with the blood of the ram.
> He offered to the Lord
The burnt offering,
> In gratitude for the gifts
He had given them and would give
> Forever and ever after.

Six

READING ARTHUR GOLD'S POEM "CHEST CANCER"

A flash of somber red
Against the Maine-drenched green,
Back of the Victory Garden,
As we kids crouched under the sun,
Weeding. It was the only sight of fox
I ever had. In the Jersey winter
I thought ah if I could have held
That fox in my line of sight.

———

On our way to have my septum removed
My father told me of the foxcub and
The Spartan boy. He meant to encourage.

I was guilty of telling the same cruel tale
To the same end, to my little girl Anna,
Who when it was over and done with asked
What did the Spartans have against pets.

But afterwards in the car when I complained
Of the hurt he held me against his chest.
So Anna holds her cat Rosette.

———

These memories and imaginations
Gnaw at my repose.

———

Anna's tenderness to Rosette,
My dad's flash of tenderness to me:
Paradise would be if I could hold them
Before not behind my eyes.

AG

"Before not behind my eyes." One thing about it
Is that the lines were written with the knowledge
That except perhaps in having the thought and also
Perhaps in writing it down in lines in a poem,

There is no Paradise behind the eyes;
And soon there would not be "before," "behind."
The thought, the line of verse, is the repose,
In which the idea of Paradise still is.

Some Paradise. Some repose. But these
Memories and imaginations that are
The way the idea of Paradise is held
Are also the fox that gnaws in the breast of repose,

Even while Arthur's carried in the father's bosom,
The bosom of Abraham. Clearly Arthur
Is also thinking of the Akedah,
In the tangle of family feeling, the cruelty,

Inadvertent and loving, which at the same time
Seems to be part of the natural scheme of things,
The tender well-meant ill-judging cruelty,
The father's story of the Spartan child,

Then Arthur's telling the story to his child.
The father telling that story is Abraham
Driving Isaac his son down to the doctor's office,
Faithful to the laws of how things are,

Except that in this poem instead of the ram
Caught in the branches there to save Isaac's life,
There is the sighting of the fox that summer,
The cancer, the bosom friend, behind the garden.

In our consenting, by the ways we spend
Our days obeying the laws of how things are,
We deliver up each other unto the God
Until one day no ram is caught in the thicket.

DF

READING ARTHUR GOLD'S "TROLLEY POEM"

         Do you
Remember slow-moving trolleys?
Do you remember men dropping
From the rear-end platforms
Of slow-moving trolleys?
So our faith in God slowly
Drops but not the monkey
On our backs, not his nails
Digging into our necks:
Guilt, justice, the desire
To be good.
              Is There No End?

          AG

God, lights flashing, bells ringing, God on his tracks,
Heading away somewhere, to some destination.

Who were the people who managed to get on board?
Where is it they were being taken to?

Arthur, yes, I remember the slow-moving trolleys;
I remember the men clinging on to the trolleys,

Clinging like monkeys not just to rear-end platforms
But hanging on by their nails just under the cables

That hooked up above to the flashing sparking lines.
A lot of fireworks, God, on your way to some station,

Rattling and clanging, making a lot of noise.
One thing you're famous for is making noise.

Then, suddenly, in the poem, God is the monkey
That rides us like the habit we can't get free of,

And for Arthur in his extremity not being able
To free himself from virtue was part of the pain;

The obligations of being what he was,
Father, and teacher, setting some kind of example.

My sister Penny at my niece's house,
The day her blood reported that the cancer

Had intensified ten times since the last report.
The obligation of being who she was,

Listening to the family pleasantries
With something like what seemed to be like pleasure.

DF

READING ARTHUR GOLD'S POEM
"ON THE BEACH AT ASBURY"

I lie halfasleep on the beach at Asbury.
The hairs on my father's chest are little tendrils of death.
The sun beating down, the murmur and susurrus of voices,
Prices of this and that, who's in, who's out, the stockmarket,
            boys' names, girls',
And behind or below the comforting murmur, faintly,
disturbed by cries,
The other clamor of the beating surf,
Felt somehow, heard somehow, through the warm sand
            and in my body as I bake
all this comes back to me now,
But especially the intricate mess of black, gray, white hair
on my father's sundarkened chest,
Not seen or touched but known,
And the sense of something coming, something dire,
hidden below or behind it all.

                    AG

Arthur knew perfectly well that this derives
From Whitman one of his fathers, and the hair
On his father's chest is the beautiful uncut hair,
The grass, that grows on graves; knew perfectly well
That in this poem he was "lying half-asleep"
In Abraham's bosom; and knew the fantasy
Of Lear that in Paradise he and his daughter
Would tell each other stories who's in who's out
And witness together the comedy of the pageant

Of lords and ladies as they pass below.
The beauty of it is that the verse proceeds,
Knowing these things, as if it didn't know them,
So "stockmarket" comes in easy, boys' names, girls' names,
The family conversation on the beach,
Everything made of common materials—
There isn't a person brought up near the ocean
Who hasn't heard around him as he lay
In safety in the family conversation,
Half-hearing it all around him, sheltered in it,
Sleeping in sunshine as if asleep in heaven,
The sound of the all-embracing sea coming in,
And that's what Arthur's poem hears all around it.
But in the last line of Arthur's poem the penultimate word
Is "it," and "it" refers, as I read it, to
The word "something," and back beyond that, his father's "chest,"
And back beyond that, the clamoring sound of the "surf."
Our death is in the beating of the surf,
"The waters of the earth gathering upon us,"
And in the beating of our father's heart,
The beating heart in Abraham's bosom, on which
There grows the beautiful grass that grows on graves.
Death's heartbeat beats in every line of the poem.

DF

READING ARTHUR GOLD'S POEM
"ROME, DECEMBER 1973"

Precious the winter light in Rome,
The year of the fuel crisis.
We walked down the middle of the Via Veneto.
You, your mother, and your aunt wore black fur coats.
Golden, the fluted columns were golden,
Visited by that light that precious light
That also as I remember touched
The stubble on a priest's face caught
In the black doorway of a church
As he was coming out upon us into the cold street
Warmed for just a moment by the precious winter light
In Rome, the year of the fuel crisis.

But at night the darkness seemed total.
Especially on a bus we took one night
Towards a destination now forgotten
The darkness outside seemed total.
Beyond the yellow balloons (lightbulbs)
Doubly reflected in the windowglass,
Beyond the wan reflected faces (our own)
We inferred a darkness so total
That even had there been children outside the bus
And even had they reached to touch the windows with their hands
We would have seen nothing,
We would not have known they were there.

We must have been going somewhere,
But all I remember now is the joking tone
Of the driver and his friend and the word

They offered when we left the bus for darkness:
"Coraggio!"

AG

For one thing there's the way the two key phrases,
"The year of the fuel crisis," "Precious the winter light"
Come fully alive with meaning in their recurrence
And make the title part of the poem itself,
"December 1973," and "Rome."
And the way this repetition gives life to
And gets it from the other repetitions
In this first stanza: "Golden, the fluted columns
were golden," and, "that light that precious light."
Not merely that certain expressions are repeated,
But that the whole stanza is saturated
With the present need for what the language looks back to
With love and longing. "The year of the fuel crisis."

The phrase makes fact of the time and realizes
Where Arthur was and who he was at the time,
And therefore what was going to become of him.
The phrases counteract the imperial claim
That poetry often praises itself by making,
The claim to sovereign synchronicity,
Possessing, gathering into itself, both past
And present, both here and there, both I
As I speak now, and that other one who once
Spoke with my voice and answered to my name.
That light that precious light but *visited*
The columns either to make them gold or show
How Rome is golden; and the light but *touched*,
And only, as Arthur remembered it, the beard

Of the priest emerging from the church-dark into
The street that was made warm *but for a moment*.

And of course there is the way, in stanza one,
That the three women enter into the poem
In accurate remembrance, the wife, the mother, the aunt,
Metonymy for the marriage, its past and future.
And they enter into the poem, as well, as if
In rehearsal for the funeral later on;
Or maybe in Arthur's mind, writing the poem,
The women in their black fur coats are the Fates,
Just as all others whom we love are Fates,
With whom we share our darkness journey toward
A forgotten destination not yet known.
The poem reads the priest in that way too.
What ceremony is he returning from?
The contrast between the dark of the church and the golden
Momentary light of the ancient street
Suggests that he's an arbiter of the dead,
Come from the place of the dead as if he were
A desert dog or other some such creature,
Come out of a long-forgotten ancient tomb,
Mercury, the shepherd of the shades.

In the second stanza the dark is everywhere,
Except for the reflections of lights in the bus,
As Arthur's poem says, or are they streetlights
Seen obscurely and as in fantasy
Through the window of the bus? Out there the golden
Faces of the children that were not there,
The putti-children—among them, as yet unborn,
Anna, his daughter and his only child,
And the bus-light reflections were also golden balloons,
As if it was a children's birthday party

In a festivity of their ignorance of death.
The grammar of this part of Arthur's sentence
is strange:
> "We inferred a darkness so total
That even had there been children outside the bus
And even had they reached to touch the windows with their hands
We would have seen nothing,
We would not have known they were there."

Strange, and the grammar allows those in the bus
To have their vision and not to have it too,
As with our every moment of being alive.
The children out there who are not there, and who
Would not have been seen had they been there, *are* there,
Nevertheless, the children we've never had,
And never will have, and the children we have had
Who are no longer children, our descendants
And ancestors, who do not reach out to touch
The lighted windows, trying to touch us, and
Who do so, in the resources of our grammar,
Is their reaching out imploring? Imploring
To be born, or tell us something, something
They know we know but that we do not know
In the way that in that other dimension, before
The event of birth or after the event of death,
They know it, though when they're born they will
Be innocent of what it was they knew?

The bus driver in Arthur's poem is Charon. As
He releases them into the dark, he says
"Coraggio" because their journey is toward
The forgotten destination not yet known.

DF

VIRGIL, *AENEID* VI

Lines 719–61

        "O father, is it
Thinkable that any spirits want to go back
From this to the upper world and once again
Into the prisons of bodies? Why do these
Poor things long so to go back to the light up there?"
Anchises answers, saying, "My son, I'll tell you,"
And he tells him in its order all the truth.

"There is a spirit that breathes and moves within
And nurtures earth and sky and ocean's wide
Savannas and the bright sphere of the moon
And Titan's star, the sun; intelligence moves
Through all there is, all things there are, and they
Are constituted by it. From this come all
The races and the kinds of men and all
The other beings; it is the life of those
That fly with wings, and those strange creatures that swim
Beneath the marbled waters of the sea.
It burns with its own pure fire in all those beings,
Until the mortality of their bodies clogs
And inhibits it. They fear, and they desire, they grieve,
And they delight, and in the shadows and
The blindnesses of what imprisons them,
Their bodies, the light's obscured. And more than that!
When they come here their souls are tainted still
With faults that are so deep inhabiting
And so corroding that they had to be punished
To eradicate these faults from them; for some
It is to be suspended upon the winds,

For others, to be washed through with flooding waters,
For others it is to be subjected to
Eviscerating fire, until at last
Their souls are purified and purged; this must
For each of us be undergone. And then at last,
When the time comes round, we are sent to Elysium.
A few of us there remain, in possession of
The blessèd fields. But, after a thousand years.
Those others you see are summoned by the god,
To drink from the river Lethe, so that in utter
Forgetfulness, willingly they will go back
Into their bodies."

READING ARTHUR GOLD'S PROSE POEM "ALLEGORY"

It's World War I. We are in the poppy-studded wheatfields of bloody Flanders. I'm enduring bloody weakening cramps and fear in a muddy trench. You're crawling recklessly under barbed wire into No Man's Land. The always unpredictable explosions, the brilliant flares, and the crackling of the Gatling gun make you laugh with delight. You have never been so deeply satisfied, so fulfilled. With my periscope I search the night for your joyous face. But the light from the flares isn't steady enough to see clearly by. Maybe I see your smile—the spaces between your teeth, your gums—but I can't be sure. I want to climb up out of the trench. I want to save your life, but I'm too fat to crawl under the wire, and too sick, anyway—too sick to move. I concentrate on enduring the pain and fear until morning. At first dawn the field falls quiet. Searching it with my periscope, I see a few poppies, some wheat graced by orange-purple light, and a familiar face. It is not quite your face. It is not quite not your face. It is your face afflicted with a bit of Lazarus. It has Lazarus's faint look of disgust, Lazarus's slightly downturned lips. We called it his rootcellar face, for it was the face he put on when he returned from his father's rootcellar, where he had to work so hard, in such wet and clammy, stinking darkness, in the years before the war. My cramps ease. I am glad to see you in life, sorry about your faint look of disgust. I throw the periscope away as you approach, bigger than any glass, spitting manfully in the blood-moistened dirt. The wheat turns yellow. The poppies renewed with sun, blood and spit, crawl towards the wire, which you with your shears cut a hole in, before passing through it to quietly assume your former position in the trench beside me, your friend, your guardian, your aging agèd father.

AG

Arthur is in his bed is in his trench
Is in his grave experiencing his nightmare.

He's lying wide awake envisioning
The fields of night. The fields of night. A phrase
That makes a beautiful meaning out of it.
But Arthur knows the meaning of it is shit.
The night is like a page not written on yet
Or it is not and it is nothing but
The chaos out there and Arthur's trying to think of it
As a page on which he could write some ordering words.
Enduring fear and bloody weakening cramps
While his brilliant child heartless in nightmare romps
Through the battlefield as if there was no death:
The daughter romps through the nightmare fields of night
To the music of the rattling Gatling guns,
As if she's Wordsworth's daughter in his great sonnet,
"If thou appear untouched by solemn thought,
The nature is not therefore less divine,
Thou dwellest in Abraham's bosom all the year,
God being with thee when we know it not."
And horrifyingly then she's Lazarus,
Come back with a look of disgust from the rootcellar dark
To be a nightmare for those who think there's no
Return from the dead. Have we returned from the dead?
Could that be one of the horrors we know about?
Disgust at what he'd been to and come back from,
Disgust at the innocence of those who haven't
Learned that in long successions they've come back,
Trailing clouds of the stink of the graves they've come from?
Our horror is our memory of the truth of it.
We come back from where, sometime before, down there,
We drank the waters of the river Lethe,
Forgetting what we had been before we went
Down there to be purified of all of that,
By death. Maybe it's true that there are those
Who can stay and picnic forever in blessed groves,

Because for them somehow the purgation is final.
But most of us had to return to the pleasures and pains
Of being here once again, not knowing exactly
What those memories are, brushed away from our bodies
In the delivery room. True dreams? False dreams?
Anna, his daughter, has come back from there,
My daughter and my son, my son-in-law,
Their little children, they have all come back
From the Underworld, bringing their DNA,
Unknowingly in their little satchel bodies
Like Aeneas bringing with him, in a satchel,
Troy, and his household gods, and watching him,
Wherever he was going, the terrible great
Gods who might turn against him any time soon.

DF

LOOKING, WHERE IS THE MAILBOX?

This fellow in the cellarage. Younger than me
When he was born, older than me now
Because he's dead and therefore has become
An ancestor in the art of what it was
Not to have been here yet or what it was
When we were here before, if only in poems
On scraps of yellowing letters written home,

The yellowing letters all of us write home,
Every day of our lives, confessing who
We were to our unforgiving parents, or
Maybe (nobody knows the truth of it)
Our forgiving parents, or our brothers and sisters,
Or wives, or children, or the lovers we had.
How now, old mole? Canst work i'th'earth so fast?

Seven

ORPHEUS AND EURYDICE

From Virgil, *Georgics* IV (lines 457–527)

> She fled from you,
> Headlong along the river, unhappy maiden,
> And did not see the frightful snake that lurked
> In the high grass, guarding the riverbank.
> The cries of the sister band of Dryads filled
> The air as high as the mountaintops; the cliffs
> Of Rhodope wept, the cliffs of Pangaea wept,
> And the warrior land of the Getae, Oríthyia, Hebrus.
> Alone upon the unfrequented shore
> Orpheus, playing his lyre, sang to himself
> His songs of you, dear wife, as day came on
> With the light of the morning sun, and as the light
> Descended in the evening. Singing he went
> Down through the very throat of Taenarus,
> The high gate of the dark kingdom of Dis,
> And through the murky grove where Terror dwells
> In black obscurity, and entered into
> The Manė's place, the place of the dreadful King
> And the hearts no human prayers can cause to pity.
>
> And, set in motion by the sound of music,
> From the lowest depths of Erebus there came,
> As numerous as the many hundred birds
> That, driven there by the coming on of evening
> Or by a winter storm, fly in for shelter
> In the foliage of a grove, the flittering shades,
> The unsubstantial phantom shapes of those
> For whom there is not any light at all—
> Women and men, famous great-hearted heroes,

The life in their hero bodies now defunct,
Unmarried boys and girls, sons whom their fathers
Had had to watch being placed on the funeral pyre,
And all around them the hideous tangling reeds
And the black ooze of Cocytos's swampy waters;
Nine times Styx wound its fettering chain around them.
And the house of Death was spellbound by his music,
All the way down to the bottom of Tártarus;
Spellbound the snakes in the hair of the Furies too;
And Cerberus the Hell-Dog's all three mouths
Were open-mouthed and silent, forgetting to bark;
The wind was still, and Ixíon's wheel stopped turning.

And now, as he was carefully going back
The way he came, and step by step avoiding
All possible wrong steps, and step by step
Eurydice, whom he was bringing back,
Unseen behind his back was following—
For this is what Proserpina had commanded—
They were coming very near the upper air,
And a sudden madness seized him, madness of love,
A madness to be forgiven if Hell but knew
How to forgive; he stopped in his tracks, and then,
Just as they were just about to emerge
Out into the light, suddenly, seized by love,
Bewildered into heedlessness, alas!
His purpose overcome, he turned, and looked
Back at Eurydice! And then and there
His labor was spilled and flowed away like water.
The implacable tyrant broke the pact: three times
The pools of Avernus heard the sound of thunder.

"What was it," she cried, "what madness, Orpheus, was it,
That has destroyed us, you and me, oh look!

The cruel Fates already call me back,
And sleep is covering over my swimming eyes.
Farewell; I'm being carried off into
The vast surrounding dark and reaching out
My strengthless hands to you forever more
Alas not yours." And saying this, like smoke
Disintegrating into air she was
Dispersed away and vanished from his eyes
And never saw him again, and he was left
Clutching at shadows, with so much still to say.
And the boatman never again would take him across
The barrier of the marshy waters of Hell.
What could he do? His wife twice taken from him.
How could he bear it? How could his tears move Hell?
The Stygian boat has carried her away,

—

And, it is said that he, day after day,
For seven months beside the river Strymon,
Sat underneath a towering cliff, and wept,
And sang, and told in song his story; entranced,
The wild beasts listened; entranced, the oak trees moved
Closer to hear the song, which was like that
Of the nightingale, in the shade of a poplar tree,
In mourning for her children who were taken,
As yet unfledged, by a herdsman, hard of heart,
Who had happened upon the nest—she weeps all night
And over and over repeats her lamentation
And fills the listening air with her sad complaint.

No thought of marriage or any other love
Could turn his heart away from its bereavement.
Alone he roamed the Hyperborean North
And wandered along the snowy banks of the Don

Or through the barren frozen fields on the sides
Of Riphaean mountains, in grief for his lost wife
And Hades' empty promise, until the enraged
Cicónian Bacchantes, in a nocturnal
Ritual orgy, tore his body to pieces
And scattered the pieces everywhere, far and wide;
And as his head, cut off from his beautiful neck,
Went tumbling down the rushing course of Hebrus,
H is voice and tongue with his last breath cried out,
"Eurydice! O poor Eurydice!"
And the banks of the downward river Hebrus echoed
"O poor Eurydice! Eurydice!"

LAKE WATER

It is a summer afternoon in October.
I am sitting on a wooden bench, looking out
At the lake through a tall screen of evergreens,
Or rather, looking out across the plane of the lake,
Seeing the light shaking upon the water
As if it were a shimmering of heat.
Yesterday, when I sat here, it was the same,
The same displaced out-of-season effect.
Seen twice it seemed a truth was being told.
Some of the trees I can see across the lake
Have begun to change, but it is as if the air
Had entirely given itself over to summer,
With the intention of denying its own proper nature.
There is a breeze perfectly steady and persistent
Blowing in toward shore from the other side
Or from the world beyond the other side.
The mild sound of the little tapping waves
The breeze has caused—there's something infantile
About it, a baby at the breast. The light
Is moving and not moving upon the water.

The breeze picks up slightly but still steadily,
The increase in the breeze becomes the mild
Dominant event, compelling with sweet oblivious
Authority alterations in light and shadow,
Alterations in the light of the sun on the water,
Which becomes at once denser and more quietly
Excited, like a concentration of emotions

That had been dispersed and scattered and now were not.
Then there's the mitigation of a cloud,
And the light subsides a little, as if into itself.
Although this is a lake it is as if
A tide were running mildly into shore.
The sound of the water so softly battering
Against the shore is decidedly sexual,
In its liquidity, its regularity,
Its persistence, its infantile obliviousness.
It is as if it had come back to being
A beginning, an origination of life.

The plane of the water is like a page on which
Phrases and even sentences are written,
But because of the breeze, and the turning of the year,
And the sense that this lake water, as it is being
Experienced on a particular day, comes from
Some source somewhere, beneath, within, itself,
Or from somewhere else, nearby, a spring, a brook,
Its pure origination somewhere else,
It is like an idea for a poem not yet written
And maybe never to be completed, because
The surface of the page is like lake water,
That takes back what is written on its surface,
And all my language about the lake and its
Emotions or its sweet obliviousness,
Or even its being like an origination,
Is all erased with the changing of the breeze
Or because of the heedless passing of a cloud.

When, moments after she died, I looked into her face,
It was as untelling as something natural,
A lake, say, the surface of it unreadable,
Its sources of meaning unfindable anymore.
Her mouth was open as if she had something to say;
But maybe my saying so is a figure of speech.

THE WHITE SKUNK

That glorious morning late in August when
The rosy-fingered dawn had scattered shadows
Away from the dreams I had dreamed the night before,
I looked out the back door of my condo, seeing
The parking lot we share, the cars we own,
And the houses all around, an embracing scene,
And there was Manfred and his small child Julia,
And, I thought for a moment, a little white toy
Trundling along behind her on its wheels.
But something was wrong with this. Julia, though little,
Wasn't so little as to be trundling such
A toy as what I thought I was seeing there,
On that glorious morning late in August when
The rosy-fingered dawn had scattered shadows.

And then I saw that the toy I thought I saw
Was not a toy but a little white skunk intently
Following Julia's legs and studying them,
And then, of course, her father had snatched her up
Into his arms, and was backing away from the skunk,
And kicking at it to get it away, but the skunk
Kept following, it seemed for a very long time,
As the three of them kept on this way on their way,
Julia crying now, a piercing cry,
And Manfred perplexed, a father protecting his child,
Backing away and saying, in a voice
Carefully calm and maybe pretending to be
Almost amused, "What should I do about this?"
Holding his child in his arms, having to keep

Backing away, unable to turn his back
On this bizarre studious creature following them.
Transfixed in the doorway of the place I live in
I stood there out of time, watching them go.

But then, as they were halfway down the driveway
The creature turned aside and disappeared
Into the tall grass alongside the driveway,
And Manfred, carrying Julia, was able to turn
And quickly make his way away from there
To the preschool across the street from the end of the driveway.
A moment later the skunk appeared again
And ran across the lawn beside our house,
Intently studying the ground, near-sighted
Creature reading the ground for information,
Moving about the yard between our house
And the kindred house next door, purposeful, wandering.
What was it trying to find? Where was it going?—
A reader of the ground as if it were.

The walls of the facility at Mount Auburn
Where she kept wandering the halls, reading blank walls
To see if there was an exit there, or maybe
A bulletin board telling her what to do,
Telling her how to be there, or where to be,
Or what she was trying to find, or where she was going,
Intently studying where it was she was.

The skunk was white where a skunk is normally black,
And striped black where it's normally striped white.
Was it transmogrified? Come up from down there
In the Underworld where it could have been changed like that?
It came back over across the lawn toward where
I was standing transfixed in the doorway of my dwelling,

Its eyes still intently studying the ground,
Close reader of the text whose narrative
Or whose instruction it was following.

Orpheus, I, stepped back in nameless fear,
As it looked as if the skunk was reading its way
Toward the back porch steps up into my condo,
Coming toward me as if it were coming home.
And then the skunk ran past my back porch steps
Reading the ground, paying no heed to me,
And disappeared in the ground cover we planted
To ornament the door yard of our dwellings
In the world the strange white skunk had disappeared from.

VIRGIL, *AENEID* VI

Lines 297–329

From here there is a road which leads to where
The waters of Tartarean Acheron are,
Where a bottomless whirlpool thick with muck
Heaves and seethes and vomits mire into
The river Cocytos. Here is the dreadful boatman
Who keeps these waters, frightful in his squalor,
Charon, the gray hairs of his unkempt beard
Depending from his chin, his glaring eyes
On fire, his filthy mantle hanging by
A loose knot from his shoulders. All by himself
He manages the sails and with his pole
Conveys the dead across in his dark boat—
He's old, but, being a god, old age is young.

A vast crowd, so many, rushed to the riverbank,
Women and men, famous great-hearted heroes,
The life in their hero bodies now defunct,
Unmarried boys and girls, sons whom their fathers
Had had to watch being placed on the funeral pyre;
As many as the leaves of the forest that,
When autumn's first chill comes, fall from the branches;
As many as the birds that flock in to the land
From the great deep when, the season, turning cold,
Has driven them over the seas to seek the sun,
They stood beseeching on the riverbank,
Yearning to be the first to be carried across,
Stretching their hands out toward the farther shore.
But the stern ferryman, taking only this one
Or this other one, pushes the rest away.

Aeneas cries out, excited by the tumult,
"O virgin, why are they crowding at the river?
What is it that the spirits want? What is it
That decides why some of them are pushed away
And others sweep across the livid waters?"
The aged priestess thus: "Anchise's son,
True scion of the gods, these are the pools
Of the river Cocytos and this the Stygian marsh,
Whose power it is to make the gods afraid
Not to keep their word. All in this crowd are helpless
Because their bodies have not been covered over.
The boatman that you see is Charon. Those
Who are being carried across with him are they
Who have been buried. It is forbidden
To take any with him across the echoing waters
That flow between these terrible riverbanks
Who have not found a resting-place for their bones.
Restlessly to and fro along these shores
They wander waiting for a hundred years.
Not until after that, the longed-for crossing."

THAT NOW ARE WILD AND DO NOT REMEMBER

Where did you go to, when you went away?
It is as if you step by step were going
Someplace elsewhere into some other range
Of speaking, that I had no gift for speaking,
Knowing nothing of the language of that place
To which you went with naked foot at night
Into the wilderness there elsewhere in the bed,
Elsewhere somewhere in the house beyond my seeking.
I have been so dislanguaged by what happened
I cannot speak the words that somewhere you
Maybe were speaking to others where you went.
Maybe they talk together where they are,
Restlessly wandering, along the shore,
Waiting for a way to cross the river.

UNTITLED DREAM POEM

What are the plants that blossom in the dark?
In my liminal dreaming waking it was green grapes
On tangled vines where some of the grapes had ripened
Nocturnally red and looking like and being

The red rear lights of cars rushing away
To get to the shore to try to get onto the boat,
And the rustle of the garments of the dead
Was the rustle of the bedsheets on the bed,

The rustle of the wandering where, the blankness
Of the faces where they meet in restaurants saying
Things to one another that do not reach
Across the tabletops, the buried dead,

Unburied till we forget them who they were.
When Adam asked the angel how they did it,
The angel blushed, his face was rosy red,
So something went on there that we can't have.

Eight

THE DEPARTURE FROM FALLEN TROY

From Virgil, *Aeneid* II (lines 704–44)

As he spoke we could hear, ever more loudly, the noise
Of the burning fires; the flood of flames was coming
Nearer and nearer. "My father, let me take you
Upon my shoulders and carry you with me.
The burden will be easy. Whatever happens,
You and I will experience it together,
Peril or safety, whichever it will be.
Little Iülus will come along beside me.
My wife will follow behind us. And you, my servants,
Listen to what I say: just as you leave
The limits of the city there is a mound,
And the vestiges of a deserted temple of Ceres,
And a cypress tree that has been preserved alive
For many years by the piety of our fathers.
We will all meet there, though perhaps by different ways
And, father, you must carry in your arms
The holy images of our household gods;
I, coming so late from the fighting and the carnage
Cannot presume to touch them until I have washed
Myself in running water." Thus I spoke.

I take up the tawny pelt of a lion and
Cover my neck and my broad shoulders with it,
And bowing down, I accept the weight of my father;
Iülus puts his hand in mine and goes
Along beside me, trying to match my steps
As best he can, trying his best to keep up.
My wife follows behind us, a little way back.
So we all set out together, making our way

Among the shadows, and I, who only just
A little while ago had faced, undaunted,
Showers of arrows and swarms of enemy Greeks,
Am frightened by every slightest change in the air
And startled by every slightest sound I hear,
Fearful for whom I walk with and whom I carry.
And just as I had almost come to the gates
And thought that I had almost gotten us free,
I thought I heard the sound of many feet,
And my father, peering intently into the shadows,
Cries out to me, "Get away, get away, my son,
My son, they are coming! I see their shining shields,
I see the glow of their weapons in the dark!"
I am alarmed, and I don't know what happened
But some power hostile to me distracts my wits
And I am confused, and I lead us away by ways
That I don't know, and off the familiar streets
That together we are following, and so,
O God! some fate has taken away my wife,
Creüsa, my wife, away from me. What happened?
Did she wander from the way that we were going?
Did she fall back, having to rest some place
Back there, and so we left her? I did not know.
I never saw her again, and as we went,
I never turned to look behind, and never
Thought of her until we reached the mound
And Ceres' ancient place. When all of us,
At last, had gotten there, we all were there,
But she had vanished and she wasn't there.
Gone from her people, gone from her child, and her husband.

TO WHERE

Wearing a tawny lion pelt upon
My spindly shoulders I carry both of them,
My father and my mother, into the darkness,
My father hoarsely singing, "They are there!"
The glimmer of something that is glimmering there—
"I see the glow of weapons in the shadows!"

Through which with my purblind eyes I think I see
Something in the darkness waiting there.
Above me in the dark my mother's voice
Calls down to me, "Who's there? Who is it there?"
Step after step together we make our way,
In the darkness of my memory of our house.

RESEMBLANCE

It was my father in that restaurant
On Central Avenue in Orange, New Jersey,
Where I stopped for lunch and a drink, after coming away
From visiting, after many years had passed,
The place to which I'd brought my father's ashes
And the ashes of my mother, and where my father's
Grandparents, parents, brothers, had been buried,
And others of the family, all together.

The atmosphere was smoky, and there was a vague
Struggling transaction going on between
The bright day light of the busy street outside,
And the somewhat dirty light of the unwashed
Ceiling globes of the restaurant I was in.
He was having lunch. I couldn't see what he was having
But he seemed to be eating, maybe without
Noticing whatever it was he may have been eating;
He seemed to be listening to a conversation
With two or three others—Shades of the Dead come back
From where they went to when they went away?
Or maybe those others weren't speaking at all? Maybe
It was a dumbshow? Put on for my benefit?

It was the eerie persistence of his not
Seeming to recognize that I was there,
Watching him from my table across the room;
It was also the sense of his being included
In the conversation around him, and yet not,

Though this in life had been familiar to me,
No great change from what had been there before,
Even in my sense that I, across the room,
Was excluded, which went along with my sense of him
When he was alive, that often he didn't feel
Included in the scenes and talk around him,
And his isolation itself excluded others.

Where were we, in that restaurant that day?
Had I gone down into the world of the dead?
Were those other people really Shades of the Dead?
We expect that, if they came back, they would come back
To impart some knowledge of what it was they had learned.
Or if this was, indeed, Down There, then they,
Down there, would reveal, to us who visit them,
In a purified language some truth that in our condition
Of being alive we are unable to know.

Their tongues are ashes when they'd speak to us.

Unable to know is a condition I've lived in
All my life, a poverty of imagination
About the life of another human being.
This is, I think, the case with everyone.
Is it because there is a silence that we
Are all of us *forbidden* to cross, not only
The silence that divides the dead from the living,
But, antecedent to that, is it the silence
There is between the living and the living,
Unable to reach across that silence through
The baffling light there always is between us?
Among the living the body can do so sometimes,
But the mind, constricted, inhibited by its ancestral

Knowledge of final separation, holds back,
Unable to complete what it wanted to say.

What is your name that I can call you by?

Virgil said, when Eurydice died again,
"There was still so much to say" that had not been said
Even before her first death, from which he had vainly
Attempted, with his singing, to rescue her.

SCRIM

I sit here in a shelter behind the words
Of what I'm writing, looking out as if
Through a dim curtain of rain, that keeps me in here.

The words are like a scrim upon a page,
Obscuring what might be there beyond the scrim.
I can dimly see there's something or someone there.

But I can't tell if it's God, or one of his angels,
Or the past, or future, or who it is I love,
My mother or father lost, or my lost sister,

Or my wife lost when I was too late to get there,
I only know that there's something, or somebody, there.
Tell me your name. How was it that I knew you?

POEM

The mind's whispering to itself is its necessity
To be itself and not to be any other,
If only for the moment as it passes.
It eats what it needs from the world around itself.
Slowly it makes its way floating through temperatures,
Degrees and other degrees of light and dark.
It moves through all things by virtue of its own
Characteristics. Mainly it is silent.
But when it utters a sound it is a sound
That others find hard to interpret, and that's known,
It supposes, only to another creature
It dreams of, so similar to itself as not
To have an entirely separate identity.
Somewhere there may be such a creature.
Emerson said: "They may be real; perhaps they are."
Yet it also thinks it's the only one, and is lonely.
It can be silent and unknown except
To itself or not even known to itself for long
Periods of time in sleepless reverie.
It is never asleep during the long nights of sleep.

THE BIRDS

They're like the birds that gather in Virgil's lines
In the park at evening, sitting among the branches,
Not knowing who it is they're sitting among,

And trying out their little songs of who
They think they are and who their mother was;
And the evening sky that seemed to be a sheltering

Presence above them guaranteed by a poem
Shifts above their heads and mutters darkly
About the weather and what is going to happen.

I don't know who it is I am sitting next to.
I can hear some notes tried out about the song
That they are trying to sing, but I don't know

What song it is, it's not exactly mine.

NOTES

The lines on the dedication page are my poem "In Eden," first published in my *Strangers: A Book of Poems* (University of Chicago Press, 1983) and then in my *Of No Country I Know: New and Selected Poems* (University of Chicago Press, 1999).

"The Intention of Things": The quotation from Goethe is from a letter to Friedrich Zelter dated 26 March 1816 (Letter 441 in *Letters from Goethe*, Edinburgh University Press, 1957, trans. M. von Herzfeld and C. Melvil Sym).

"Brunswick, Maine, Early Winter, 2000": This poem is dedicated to the memory of William L. Moran.

"Reading Arthur Gold's Poem 'On the Beach at Asbury'": "The waters of the earth gathering upon us" derives from Wordsworth, *The Prelude*, v, line 130.

"Poem": Emerson said, "They may be real; perhaps they are," in his great essay "Experience."